WELCOME TO

YELLOWSTONE

NATIONAL PARK

MAP KEY

The maps throughout this
book use the following icons:

 Bear Viewing Area

 Bison Viewing Area

 Campground

 Driving Excursion

 Elk Viewing Area

Hiking Trail

 Lodging

 Point of Interest

Ranger Station

 Visitor Center

About National Parks

A national park is an area of land that has been set aside by Congress. National parks protect nature and history. In most cases, no hunting, grazing, or farming is allowed. The first national park in the United States—and in the world—was Yellowstone National Park. It is located in parts of Wyoming, Idaho, and Montana. It was founded in 1872. In 1916, the U.S. National Park Service began.

Today, the National Park Service manages more than 380 sites. Some of these sites are historic, such as the Statue of Liberty or Martin Luther King, Jr. National Historic Site. Other park areas preserve wild land. The National Park Service manages 40% of the nation's wilderness areas, including national parks. Each year, millions of people from around the world visit these national parks. Visitors may camp, go canoeing, or go for a hike. Or, they may simply sit and enjoy the scenery, wildlife, and the quiet of the land.

VISITOR GUIDES

TABLE OF

The Child's World®

Published in the United States of America by The Child's World®

PO Box 326
Chanhassen, MN 55317-0326
800-599-READ
www.childsworld.com

Acknowledgements
The Child's World®: Mary Berendes, Publishing Director

The Design Lab: Kathleen Petelinsek, Design and Page Production

Map Hero, Inc.: Matt Kania, Cartographer

Red Line Editorial: Bob Temple, Editorial Direction

Photo Credits
Cover and this page: Roger Ressmeyer/Corbis

Interior: Annie Griffiths Belt/Corbis: 16–17; BrandXPictures: 7, 9; Dave G. Houser/Post-Houserstock/Corbis: 21; Frank Lane Picture Agency/Corbis: 2–3; Geoffrey Clements/Corbis: 24; George Steinmetz/Corbis: 23 (bottom); Jeff Vanuga/Corbis: 1, 13 (right); Jonathan Blair/Corbis: 26; Kevin R. Morris/Corbis: 27; Lester Lefkowitz/Corbis: 15; Michael T. Sedam/Corbis: 10; PhotoDisc: 23 (top); Scott T. Smith/Corbis: 13 (left); Wolfgang Kaehler/Corbis: 19,

Library of Congress Cataloging-in-Publication Data
Temple, Teri.
  Welcome to Yellowstone National Park / by Teri Temple and Bob Temple.
    p. cm. — (Visitor guides)
  Includes index.
  ISBN 1-59296-703-5 (library bound : alk. paper)
  1. Yellowstone National Park–Juvenile literature.
  I. Temple, Bob. II. Title. III. Series.
  F722.T46 2006
  917.87'5202–dc22   2005030070

On the cover and this page
Yellowstone's Great Fountain Geyser erupts about once every 10 hours. It usually sends water about 100 feet (30 m) into the air, but has also been known to shoot bursts up to 230 feet (70 m).

On page 1
The ground around Crater Hills Geyser is covered with small knobby deposits of geyserite (GY-zer-ite). The geyser's hot water carries geyserite up from underground, and the knobs form when the water cools.

On pages 2–3
Yellowstone's Madison River is a favorite stop for visitors who enjoy fly fishing.

WELCOME TO YELLOWSTONE NATIONAL PARK

▲

CONTENTS

🚶‍♂️🚶

The First Park

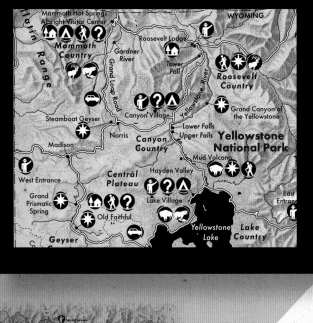

W elcome to Yellowstone National Park! Yellowstone was the first national park in America. It lies mostly in Wyoming, but creeps into Montana and Idaho, too.

Yellowstone is a big place to explore. It is home to the world's largest collection of **geysers** and **hot springs**. Winding trails, towering pines, and sparkling streams are all around. Yellowstone is the natural habitat for more plants and animals than anywhere else in the lower 48 states.

Our trip will take us through five very different regions. We will follow the Grand Loop Road. It is a 142-mile (229 km) route that runs through the park. We'll find simmering **mud pots**, wandering bison, and exploding geysers. So grab a park ranger, hop on a horse, or get in your car. Let's spend a day in the park!

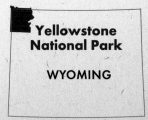

Yellowstone National Park

WYOMING

Located in Yellowstone Lake, Fishing Cone is a popular spot for visitors. This hot spring got its name in the 1870s, when it was discovered that you could catch a fish in the lake, and then swing it into the hot cone and cook your fish while it was still on the hook! Today's visitors can only look at the cone—fishing (and cooking) there are no longer allowed.

Mammoth Country

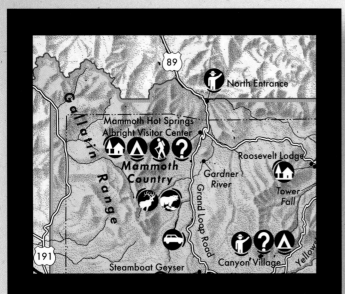

Mammoth Country is home to the Mammoth Hot Springs. Here, hot water full of **minerals** bubbles to the surface from deep below. For thousands of years, these springs have formed beautiful limestone **terraces** and colorful pools.

Maybe you'd like to take a dip in the "Boiling River." This large hot spring enters the Gardner River in Mammoth Country. Hot and cold waters mix in pools along the river's edge. Bathers swim while large clouds of steam drift overhead.

Shoshone Sheep Eaters

People have lived in the area that is now Yellowstone National Park for more than 10,000 years. That's since the end of the last ice age! Lodgepole pine forests and aspen groves were just beginning to grow then. Animals like elk, bison, black bears, coyotes, and bighorn sheep soon moved in. A small group of Shoshone Native Americans first made this place home. They were known as "sheep eaters." This **nomadic** tribe hunted big horn sheep as its main source of food.

Minerva Terrace is one of the most visited areas in the Mammoth Hot Springs area. The terraces get their bright colors from bacteria and algae in the water. Springs that have dried-up are white or gray.

🚶 Named for the tower-shaped peaks of rock nearby, Tower Fall is where Tower Creek joins the Yellowstone River. Like other waterfalls in the park, Tower Fall is best seen in the spring, when higher water levels (from rain and melting snow) cause the water to roar over the edge.

Roosevelt Country

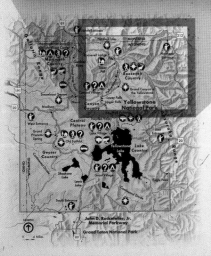

Roosevelt Country might make you feel like you are in the Old West. You might even see a stagecoach! You could travel by horseback to an Old West cookout with some rootin' tootin' entertainment at Yancey's Hole. You could also follow the Bannock Trail, an old Native American route that meanders through the rolling hills.

One of the area's favorite sites is the stunning Tower Fall. The 132-foot (40-m) falls is surrounded by lofty volcanic peaks. It is one of the most well-known sites in Yellowstone.

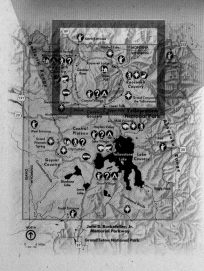

Next, we stop to visit some ancient plants and trees that have been turned to stone. They were buried in volcanic ash from past eruptions. The heat and ash preserved the trees for millions of years, turning the wood into stone. The best spot to see these **petrified** trees is at Specimen Ridge.

Be on the lookout for gray wolves! They make their home in the forests here. On a cold wintry day, you may get an extra chill as you hear the call of a wolf.

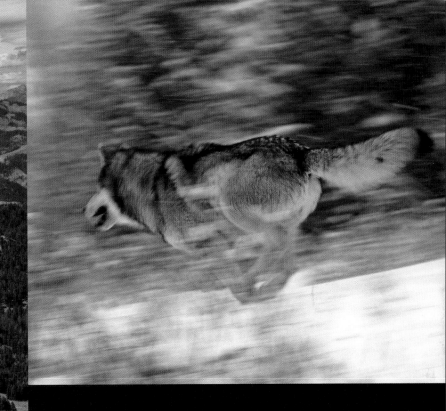

Return of the Gray Wolf

Long ago, gray wolves roamed through Yellowstone. However, they quickly disappeared in the early 1900s, because people hunted them. The gray wolf became an endangered species. Their howls had been missing from the park for decades. Today, officials are working to help the gray wolf population thrive here. In 1996, 31 gray wolves were released into the park. The wolf population is growing once again. Now you may once again hear the call of the gray wolf.

 This petrified redwood tree was burned by volcanic ash more than 50 million years ago. Yellowstone's petrified trees are unusual because many of them remained upright.

Canyon Country

As we take the Grand Loop south, we come to a breathtaking sight. The stormy Yellowstone River begins in Yellowstone Lake. It winds through roughly 20 miles (32 km) of the Grand **Canyon** of Yellowstone. It roars and crashes through the towering cliffs and cascades over two major waterfalls.

The waterfalls flow over volcanic rock that is resistant to erosion. The Upper Falls is 109 feet (33 m) of plunging water. It is very impressive, but its partner is even bigger. The Lower Falls, at 308 feet (94 m), is the centerpiece of Canyon Country.

For brave visitors, the best view of the falls is down "Uncle Tom's Trail." More than 300 steps and several downhill slopes bring you down 500 feet (152 m) into the canyon. There, you can hear the thunderous roar of the Lower Falls. You can feel its power!

The Grand Canyon of Yellowstone is one of the most well known areas in the park. It is between 800 and 1,200 feet (244 and 366 m) deep and around 1,500 to 4,000 feet (457 to 1,219 m) wide. The canyon has been featured in thousands of drawings and paintings, including the famous 1872 painting by Thomas Moran (seen on page 24).

Bison

Imagine that as you drive through Yellowstone, you see an enormous animal. As you pull up to it, you see that it's as tall as your car and almost as long. What is this massive animal? It's the bison, often called buffalo by mistake. Bison once roamed the West by the millions. They were almost hunted to extinction in the 1800s. They have since found a safe home in Yellowstone. They can be seen lumbering around Firehole River or in Hayden Valley.

Bison are the largest land animals in North America. They often stand over 6 feet (2 m) high at the shoulder and can weigh over 1,800 pounds (816 kg).

As you leave Canyon Country, take a leisurely drive through Hayden Valley. It was an old lake bed formed during the last ice age. Wildlife abounds here. Trumpeter swans and Canada geese hang out in marshy areas. Bison, elk, and deer graze in the meadows. Some even approach the road. They may come near your car. Make sure to stay back, however. The animals may look friendly, but they are still wild animals. They can be dangerous to people.

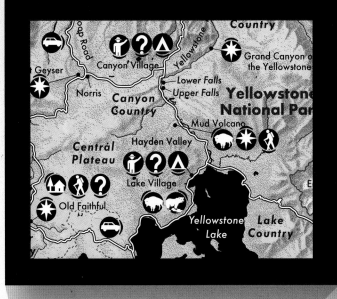

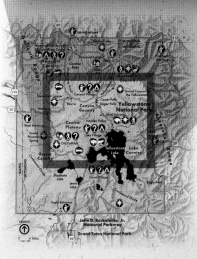

Mud Volcano Trail

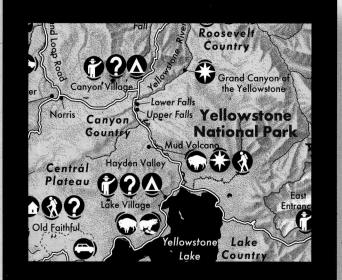

It's time for an interesting and smelly side trip. Sound like fun? If so, stop in the Mud Volcano area between Canyon Country and Lake Country. Here you will see pools filled with hot, muddy water. The trees have been cooked by steam. You will also smell strange odors created by the unique landforms.

A huge volcano erupted in this area about 640,000 years ago. At Mud Volcano Trail, you are close to one of the vents from which that lava flowed. These vents are still active. Scientists watch them for future volcanic eruptions.

The mud pots of this area are created by a kind of gas. Tiny creatures use this gas as food. They turn the gas into sulfuric acid. It smells like rotten eggs. This smelly acid breaks down the rock until it is a wet clay mud. Steam and other gases explode through the mud. The gray blobs bubble and boil.

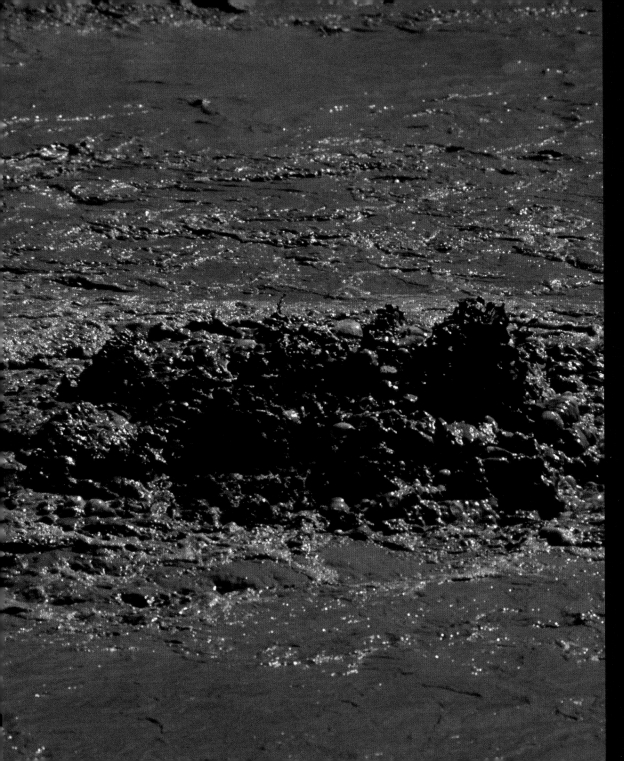

The Dragons of Mud Volcano Trail

Visitors love the Dragon's Mouth and the Black Dragon's Cauldron. The Dragon's Mouth gets its name from the spray of water that comes out of a cave like a dragon's lashing tongue. The belch of steam looks like his fiery breath. The Black Dragon's Cauldron is a pool with turbulent bubbles at one end. The bubbles make visitors wonder if the dragon is lurking just below the surface!

Lake Country

Yellowstone Lake is the main attraction in Lake Country. The lake sits in a large crater that was formed by a volcano. Melting glaciers more than 12,000 years ago filled the crater with water.

At 136 square miles (352 sq km), the lake is so large that it can create its own weather. Its tree-lined shore and deep, blue waters make the perfect home for wildlife. Moose, bear, osprey, and bald eagles live here. With plenty of streams flowing into it, the lake provides an abundance of fish, including the native cutthroat trout.

Here visitors can choose a variety of activities to fill their days. Take a scenic cruise to view the wildlife. Go on a fishing expedition. Try your hand at fly fishing in Yellowstone River or one of the many streams that feed the lake.

Isa Lake

Isa Lake lies more than 8,000 feet (2,438 m) above sea level, along the **Continental Divide**. As a result, its water flows into both the Atlantic and Pacific Oceans! It is the only lake in the world to do this—and it does it backwards! The west side of the lake flows into the Firehole River. Its waters eventually reach the Atlantic. In the spring, the east side of the lake runs into the Snake River. Those waters end in the Pacific. What an amazing lake!

Geyser Country

Mud pots, hot pools, and **fumaroles** can be found in Geyser Country. But it's the geysers that people come to see. The most famous geyser of all is Old Faithful.

Old Faithful has not missed the opportunity to erupt in more than 120 years. Every 92 minutes or so, Old Faithful releases thousands of gallons of steaming water toward the sky. This fountain of water can last up to five minutes. It can reach as high as 184 feet (56 m)! Nathaniel Langford helped name this geyser on an expedition in 1870. Because it was so reliable in its eruptions, his group called it "Old Faithful."

While here, make sure to check out the historic Old Faithful Inn. It was built in the winter of 1903-04. It is made of local logs and stone. They can still be seen in the beautiful lobby.

Just before it erupts, the water at Old Faithful reaches temperatures of more than 200 F (93 C). Old Faithful is the most popular attraction in all of Yellowstone—and it's not even one of the biggest geysers!

Grand Prismatic Spring is almost 370 feet (113 m) across and about 160 feet (49 m) deep. This hot spring—the center is 188 F (87 C)— is known for its bright colors, which are caused by bacteria. Each type of bacteria has its own color, and each type lives at different temperatures.

23

The Hayden Expedition

In 1871, Dr. Ferdinand Hayden led an expedition to explore the Yellowstone area. His friend Nathaniel P. Langford suggested the trip. Langford was a business-man who had traveled there. He would be instrumental in establishing Yellowstone as a national park.

Hayden's expedition was not the first of its kind. But it was unique, because he included artists and photographers in his group. They made stunning paintings and took photographs. It provided proof

for the government that the natural wonders of Yellowstone existed. It was clear the land should be protected. The expedition was a success!

At the time, there were no national parks. In 1872, President Ulysses S. Grant signed a law declaring Yellowstone the first national park. He said it would forever be "dedicated and set apart as a public park or pleasuring ground for the benefit and enjoyment of the people."

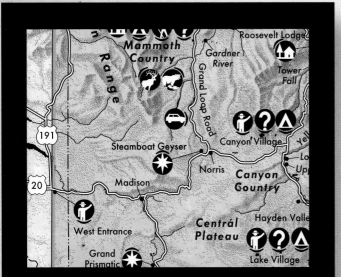

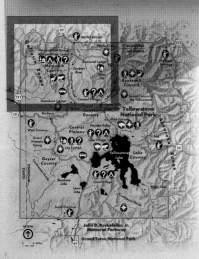

Geyser Country has thousands of other **hydrothermal** sights to see. Steamboat Geyser is just a short ways north in the Norris Geyser **Basin**. It is the world's tallest geyser, reaching heights of 300 feet (91 m). But it's a rare sight to see—not nearly as predictable as Old Faithful. At Midway Geyser Basin is Grand Prismatic Spring, Yellowstone's largest hot spring. Take time to enjoy the beautiful colors nature has produced there. Whatever you choose to look at, Geyser Country will not disappoint you!

Lodgepole Pine Forest Fire of 1988

Yellowstone is home to a majestic forest of lodgepole pines. In the summer of 1988, lightning caused several wildfires to start in the park. The weather was extremely dry, and for several weeks, the fires grew. Crews worked hard to contain them. On August 20, the wind picked up. More of the park burned on that day than ever before. That day would come to be called "Black Saturday."

No one had ever seen a fire burn like that in Yellowstone. Scientists were not surprised, however. They knew it was natural for a fire like this to happen. These fires happen about once every 300 years. In fact, the lodgepole pine needs fire! Its pine cones are so tough, they need the heat of fire to pop open. When they pop, they drop the seeds for a new generation of trees. For this forest, the fire was as natural as the rain and the sun.

This 1995 photo shows all of the new plant and tree life that grew after the 1988 fire. Because of ash left by the fire, many of the seeds benefitte[d]
[s]oil. The fire also burned down tall trees that would have shaded the new trees. The young trees could now receive the sunlight they needed to g[row]

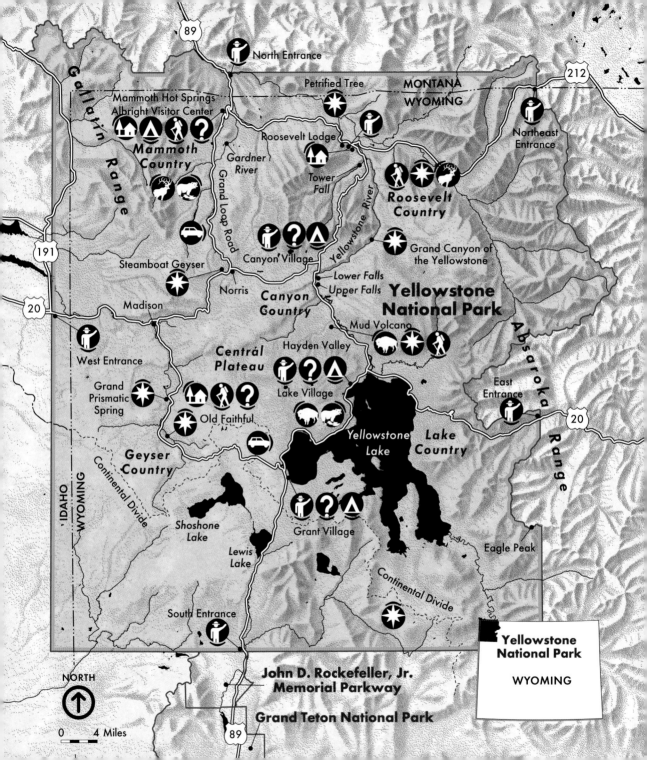

89

North Entrance

Petrified Tree

MONTANA
WYOMING

212

Mammoth Hot Springs
Albright Visitor Center

Roosevelt Lodge

Northeast
Entrance

*Mammoth
Country*

Gardner
River

Tower
Fall

*Roosevelt
Country*

191

Grand Loop Road

Steamboat Geyser

Canyon Village

Yellowstone River

Grand Canyon of
the Yellowstone

Norris

Lower Falls
Upper Falls

**Yellowstone
National Park**

Madison

*Canyon
Country*

20

Mud Volcano

*Central
Plateau*

Hayden Valley

Absaroka Range

West Entrance

Lake Village

East
Entrance

20

Grand
Prismatic
Spring

Old Faithful

*Geyser
Country*

*Yellowstone
Lake*

*Lake
Country*

Continental Divide

IDAHO
WYOMING

Grant Village

Shoshone
Lake

Lewis
Lake

Eagle Peak

Continental Divide

South Entrance

NORTH

0   4 Miles

John D. Rockefeller, Jr.
Memorial Parkway

89

Grand Teton National Park

**Yellowstone
National Park**

WYOMING

YELLOWSTONE NATIONAL PARK FAST FACTS

Date founded: March 1, 1872

Location: Northwest corner of Wyoming. Very small areas also spill into Montana and Idaho.

Size: 3,472 square miles/8,992 sq km; 2,222,080 acres/899,244 hectares

Major habitats: Forest, grasslands, lakes, and rivers

Important landforms: An active volcano, one of the world's largest calderas (crater), 10,000 thermal features including more than 300 geysers, and more than 290 waterfalls

Elevation:
    Highest: 11,358 feet/3,462 m (Eagle Peak)
    Lowest: 5,282 feet/1,610 m (Reese Creek)

Weather:
    Average yearly rainfall: From 10 inches/25 cm to to 80 inches/203 cm depending on the area
    Average temperatures: 9 F/-13 C to 80 F/27 C
    Highest: 98 F/37 C (Lamar 1936)
    Lowest: -66 F/-54 C (Madison 1933)

Number of animal species: 59 species of mammals, 311 kinds of birds, 18 species of fish, 6 reptile species, and 4 kinds of amphibians

Main animal species: Bison, elk, moose, pronghorn, black bear, grizzly bear, coyote, osprey, and trumpeter swan

Main plant species: Lodgepole pine, Engelmann spruce, fairy slipper orchid, Indian paintbrush, and yellow monkey flower

Number of endangered or threatened animal/plant species: 4—gray wolf, bald eagle, lynx, and grizzly bear

Native people: Shoshone (A total of 26 Native American tribes are officially affiliated with the park.)

Number of visitors each year: About 3 million

Important sites and landmarks: Geysers (especially Old Faithful), 290 waterfalls, Norris Geyser Basin, Yellowstone Lake, Gallatin Range, Hayden Valley, Yellowstone Canyon, the Petrified Forests

Tourist activities: Ranger-led tours and programs, sightseeing tours, fishing, boating, horseback riding, biking, hiking, cross-country skiing, and snowmobiling

GLOSSARY

basin (BAY-sin): A basin is a hollow in the surface of the land. Bison roam across the basin. Bison sometimes roam across shallow basins at Yellowstone.

canyon (KAN-yun): A canyon is a deep narrow valley with steep sides. It usually has a stream or river flowing through it. The Yellowstone River runs through the Grand Canyon of the Yellowstone.

Continental Divide (kon-tih-NEN-tull dih-VYD): The Continental Divide is an imaginary line where the waters that flow into the Pacific Ocean (west) and the Atlantic Ocean (east) meet. Settlers crossed the Continental Divide in Yellowstone as they traveled west.

fumaroles (FYOO-muh-rohlz): Fumaroles are "dry geysers" that are created when water vapor of gas escapes out of holes in the ground. The fumaroles in Yellowstone can be so strong that they make roaring sounds like thunder and the earth trembles.

geysers (GY-zerz): Geysers are special hot springs that erupt with fountains of water. These eruptions are the result of increased pressure in hot water that was trapped underground. Old Faithful, in Yellowstone, is the most famous geyser in the world.

hot springs (HOT SPRINGZ): Hot springs are flows of water that have been heated by lava beneath the Earth's surface. The hot springs in Yellowstone are many colors because of water temperature, algae, microscopic creatures, or minerals.

hydrothermal (hy-druh-THERM-ull): Hydrothermal refers to the activity that happens when water from on top of the earth sinks into the ground and meets the hot lava underground. There are lots of hydrothermal springs in Yellowstone National Park.

minerals (MIN-er-ullz): Minerals are the building blocks of rock. They include such solid substances are diamonds, graphite, and salt. Minerals help color the hot springs in Geyser Country.

mud pots (MUD POTS): Mud pots are another type of hot spring. They form when the hot water mixes with clay and other substances. Some mud pots in Canyon Country smell like rotten eggs.

nomadic (noh-MAD-ik): People are nomadic when they roam from place to place in search of food and supplies. The Shoshone "sheepeaters" of Yellowstone's past were a nomadic tribe.

petrified (PET-rih-fyd): If a living thing, like a tree, gets soaked with water and minerals, over time it will become as hard as stone. When that happens it is called petrified. You can see petrified trees in Roosevelt Country.

terraces (TAYR-ess-ez): Terraces are sets of step-like surfaces that were made by the hot springs. You will see many terraces in Geyser Country around the hot springs.

TO FIND OUT MORE

FURTHER READING

Justesen, Kim Williams and Judy Newhouse (illustrator).
"Hey Ranger!" Kids Ask Questions about Yellowstone National Park.
Guilford, CT: Falcon, 2005.

Patent, Dorothy Hinshaw and William Muñoz (photographer).
Yellowstone Fires: Flames and Rebirth.
New York: Holiday House, 1990.

Petersen, David.
Yellowstone National Park.
New York: Children's Press, 2001.

ON THE WEB

Visit our home page for lots of links about
Yellowstone National Park:

http://www.childsworld.com/links

NOTE TO PARENTS, TEACHERS, AND LIBRARIANS:
We routinely check our Web links to make sure
they're safe, active sites—so encourage your
readers to check them out!

INDEX